D0394831

365

WAYS TO
SAY I LOVE YOU

365 Ways to Say I Love You

© Cover photograph left: Getty Images/Bavaria (Jacques Copeau)

Copy editing: MediText, Stuttgart
Text: Christopher Dörries
Translation: Beate Gorman
Photos: Adobe Image Library (17); Creative Collection (3); Digital Stock (5); Digital Vision (2); MEV (8); Photo Alto (8); PhotoDisc (8); Project Photos (6); Stockbyte (6)

© 2002 DuMont monte Verlag, Köln
(Dumont monte UK, London)

All rights reserved

The advice given in this book has been subjected to careful consideration and examination by the author, the editors and the publishers; nevertheless, no guarantee can be given. No liability can be assumed by the author, the editors, the publishers or their agents for personal injury, material damage or financial loss.

ISBN 3-8320-7098-2
Printed in Slovenia

Contents

The first declaration of love

When you are in love, you would obviously like the other person to reciprocate these feelings. But how, if the other person doesn't know that he or she is the centre of your loving affections? The solution: pluck up courage and confess your love. Such a first declaration of love can be done in a multitude of ways, and you will have to decide yourself which one is the right one for you.

1

It is important when making your first declaration of love that you find just the right words. If the object of your desire doesn't like poetry, you shouldn't try and declare your love in the form of a poem. Think carefully what might impress your beloved.

2

For your first declaration of love you should pay
attention to your outer appearance. That doesn't mean
that you can't wear casual and informal clothes, but
you should make sure that your clothes are neat and clean
and that you make a good impression.

3

Look for a suitable setting for your declaration of love. While you are still at school, it might be all right to declare your love to the object of your desire on the bus or in the street, but when you are a little older, you should choose a special place if possible. A romantic restaurant or the beach or park could be such a suitable place.

4

In some cases you won't have the opportunity to choose a suitable place for your declaration of love – perhaps because time is of the essence. However, in such cases you should at least attach importance to an imaginative and creative declaration.

5

The best time for a declaration of love is of course the evening, because you will have some time for yourselves afterwards. Of course, you could also declare your love in the morning, but remember: if you then have to go your separate ways, perhaps because you have to go to the office, it can be very unsatisfactory for both of you.

6

Invite your beloved to dinner in a romantic restaurant – perhaps for a candlelight dinner? In the glow of the candles look deeply into her/his eyes. Then simply say "I love you." There is no need for any further explanation.

7

Maybe there are musicians in the restaurant – as is customary in many southern countries – who will play a love song at the table if asked to do so. Or you could hire one or two musicians for a brief appearance (you should, however, ask the manager for his permission beforehand). Maybe they could play Stevie Wonder's "I just called to say I love you" or something similarly expressive. When the last notes have been played and you have your "peace and quiet" again, you can tell the person opposite that you wanted to express your feelings for him or her through this song.

8

Of course, you could also go to a restaurant where flower sellers regularly come to the tables. Depending on your financial situation, you should buy one or all of the red roses and hand them to your beloved – perhaps with the words, "These flowers express what I feel for you."

9

It is also romantic to declare your love at the place where you first met – at least if it is a place that is suitable for a declaration of love. A train station, for example, might be suitable, but perhaps not a discotheque, because of the loud music (unless you can convince the owner to let you in before the official opening time).

10

If you declare your love at the place where you first met, you could indicate the significance of the moment when you first laid eyes on your beloved. Of course, you could also say what you felt if it was love at first sight.

11

One thing is very important for your declaration of love: don't stare at the floor, the ceiling or anywhere else – look straight into the eyes of the person that you love. Maybe you could also take his or her hand – this creates an additional physical bond.

Love starts with the eyes.
(Russian saying)

12

13

Of course you could also declare your love at home. However, this might not be the most suitable place. After all, it is your very own terrain, and the person you love might feel uneasy giving you the brush-off at your own place if he or she does not share your feelings – something that hopefully will not happen.

14

An especially nice way of declaring your love: give the person that you love a cuddly toy as a present. Attach a letter with the words, "This bear (or lamb or whatever toy you have chosen) is to be envied. From now on, it will spend all its time just with you. I would like to change places with it, but maybe your heart is big enough for both of us? I love you." Of course, you should be present when the letter is opened and read.

15

Are you already fairly certain that your feelings are reciprocated, and do you like to travel? Great! Present your beloved with a voucher for a weekend trip to Paris, the capital of love, adding, "If you love me as much as I love you, we should celebrate our love. And what better place than the capital of love?"

Music is another good means of telling someone "I love you." Record a cassette with love songs that you especially like and give it to your beloved with the words, "This music expresses what you mean to me."

16

17

A declaration of love of a very special kind (only suitable for people with a sense of humour): first of all, list your beloved's faults and weaknesses – especially those that he or she has admitted to. Then show with words (maybe with a quote?) or gestures (for example, with an ardent kiss) that you love him or her with all his or her weaknesses and faults.

He does not love,
who does not consider the faults of his beloved
to be virtues.
(Johann Wolfgang von Goethe)

19

Do you have musical talent? Why not compose and write a love song for your beloved, record it on cassette and give to him or her as a present? Maybe you even have the opportunity of copying the song onto a CD.

20

A picture you have painted yourself is bound to be accepted as a wonderful declaration of love. Of course, the motif should fit the occasion. For example you could paint Cupid, the god of love, hitting you with an arrow bearing the name of your beloved.

21

Write a love poem and hand it to the person you love. Poems might be perceived as old-fashioned these days, but if someone goes to the trouble of writing one, it is always something special.

A very daring declaration of love: give the object of your desires an erotic photo of yourself and say, "If you like, what you see on this photo can be all yours."

23

Another declaration of love with a photo: make a collage from two photos of yourself. On the one picture you should look sad and on the other very cheerful. Above the first photo write, "This is how I feel without you," and above the second one, "This is how I feel when you are near me." Present this declaration of love personally to your object of desire.

Don't be afraid to declare your love.
You don't need to fear that you will make
a fool of yourself. Even if the other person
brushes you off (which hopefully will not
happen), you can be sure that he or she
will feel flattered and won't laugh at you.

As a hint, you could give the person you love a love story (such as "Romeo and Juliet") in which you write a dedication which on the one hand says something about your feelings, and on the other hand relates to the novel. In regard to "Romeo and Juliet" this dedication could be, "This love story ends tragically, but I'm sure this won't happen to ours."

Younger people might give each other a video with a love story like "Titanic", for example. You should watch the film together with your beloved – you will often get close to one another without the need for words.

26

27

Of course, the cinema is also a suitable place to show the other person your love. Go and see a romantic film together and during the love scenes take his or her hand furtively into yours. If the reaction is positive, you can probably soon hope for the first kiss.

28

Have a party. Make sure that at least one slow song is played. Ask the person you love to dance with you and carefully get closer to him or her. If the response is positive, you can whisper your feelings into his or her ear while you are dancing.

29

Here's a somewhat unusual idea for declaring your love: lease a billboard near where your beloved lives and deliver your message of love there. A word of advice: make sure beforehand that the partner of your dreams would appreciate such a public declaration of love.

30

Declare your love to your dream partner through an advertisement in the newspaper. It should be placed amongst the family ads and say what you feel. If you don't want to make the real name of your beloved public you could use his or her nickname.

31

Young people with little money could place an ad amongst the classifieds – almost every newspaper offers a low-price classified ad market once a week. There is usually a category such as "Family ads", "Congratulations" or similar where a declaration of love can be placed. You should, however, make sure that the partner of your dreams actually reads these ads.

32

Declare your love using the words of famous poets. No matter whether you give the partner of your dreams a love poem in writing or recite it yourself: the words of famous people are often more appropriate than our own. So why not make use of them?

33

There is no doubt:
Thousands will worship you;
But to love you
– Only my heart can do this.
(Jean-Jacques Rousseau)

34

I think of you
when the sun
reflects on the sea;
I think of you
when the moonshine
paints its glow in the springs.
(Johann Wolfgang von Goethe)

35

For people who like to dress up: look for a declaration of love in a play, put on the suitable clothes and recite this declaration of love to the object of your desires – of course with the appropriate dramatic gestures!

36

At the cinema, regional advertising is often screened before the main feature. Commission a short spot (a sign with the words "I love you, ... Yours, ..." is often enough) and have it screened. Then invite your ideal partner to the cinema and wait for his or her response.

.

37

For men: buy a piece of jewellery such as a ring or an attractive necklace and present it to the woman of your dreams. Jewellery often tells her what you feel for her.

Give Mr. Right one of those kids'
books where drawings and short sentences
describe in a delightful manner how
one rabbit loves the other rabbit, for
example. A short dedication can explain
your feelings, if necessary.

38

Hearts are the symbol of love. Bake a cake in the shape of a heart for him or give her a gingerbread heart at the local fair. You won't need many more words to say what you feel.

39

40

For men: shoot down a rose at the shooting gallery at the fair and hand it to the woman of your dreams with the words, "A rose for the most beautiful rose that I know." Everything else will work out on its own ...

41

Often the direct way is best with a declaration of love: simply tell your beloved – at the right moment – that you would like to kiss him or her. The response will show you where you stand.

42

For young people: a declaration of love via
SMS can be a good way of expressing your feelings
if you are too afraid to talk directly with your
ideal partner. Maybe you will soon receive an SMS
in return with a similar statement.

43

Today, a declaration of love via e-mail isn't necessarily perceived
as a faux pas. You could attach a file to your e-mail with an expressive
piece of music, a fitting cartoon or a photo of yourself. You might
even find the right words for a love letter on the Internet, or you could
have someone else write a love letter for you (of course, it is much better
if you write the letter yourself).

44

If you're sending a love letter via e-mail, you should only send it to your beloved's private address. At work, e-mails are unfortunately often opened by colleagues, and this could be rather embarrassing for the person of your dreams.

45

Another humorous way of declaring your love: have the following text printed on a T-shirt in your size: "(beloved's name), I love you!" Wear this shirt the next time you meet your beloved. Your declaration of love will be hard to miss!

46

You could also show your love with body painting. Have the following message written on your torso, arm or any other place that is visible to the partner of your dreams: "I love you, (beloved's name)." Face the other person and wait for his or her response.

47

If you like public appearances, you could ask the DJ at a discotheque if you could say a brief message over the microphone. Then explain your love for him or her for everyone to hear.

48

A declaration of love in true regal style: dress up as a prince or princess and ask your beloved in old-fashioned words to be your Queen/King of Hearts and spend your future life together.

49

Invite him or her for a trip to the mountains. Look for a quiet spot with a good echo. Shout out your love so loud that it is echoed. Make sure it is a nice sunny day – a trip like this is not very romantic in the rain.

50

Even if your knees are trembling, don't give yourself Dutch courage before your declaration of love. It is not particularly considerate to declare your love while smelling of alcohol, and your chance of rejection would only be increased.

51

Do you have a talent for drama? Maybe you could present your declaration of love as a pantomime! You should rehearse this in front of a mirror so that your declaration will be understandable to the partner of your dreams.

52

A culinary declaration of love, also suitable for unskilled cooks: invite the person you love for a meal, cook noodles in the shape of letters and write "I love you" on the plate. Afterwards you could go somewhere else for a meal if you wish. But perhaps you will then have an appetite for something different?

53

You could also cook spaghetti and write "I love you" with ketchup on a separate plate. However, you should also prepare another sauce because pasta and ketchup are not necessarily everybody's idea of a gourmet meal.

Another form of a culinary declaration of love: bake a heart-shaped cake on which you write with icing, "I love you, (beloved's name)". Present it to the man or woman of your desire at the next suitable opportunity (however, other people shouldn't be present then; after all, your love only concerns you and the partner of your dreams).

54

55

Do you know members of a band or a choir? Ask them if they would be prepared to play or sing a serenade at the front door of your beloved's house. Of course it should be a love song!

56

Congratulations performed as a song are nothing unusual these days. There are even service companies that offer this. Maybe you could employ such a messenger of happiness to have your declaration of love conveyed as a song.

57

Hackneyed, but nevertheless effective: give the partner of your dreams a large bunch of roses to tell him or her, "I love you!" Of course, the roses should be red and long-stemmed, if possible. Do it in style – the bunch should definitely not be too small!

58

In a declaration of love, you don't always need to say the words "I love you." You could declare your love in a more poetic way, for example, "I feel more for you than there are stars in the sky."

More poetic declarations of love: "You are the only person in the whole world who is really important to me", "Without you my life is dull and grey", "Only when I am with you does the sun really shine."

59

60

You can also declare your love without words – with a tender touch, an affectionate kiss or some action that is meaningful to the other person. However, this gesture must be appropriate to the situation, so that the other person perceives it as it is intended.

61

Apart from love at first sight,
there is love at first touch.
This might go deeper still.
(Vladimir Nabokov)

To love is the delight
Of beholding and touching
A loveable and loving creature.
(Stendhal)

62

63

Play the old game "He/she loves me, he/she loves me not" with your beloved in a meadow covered in daisies. Make sure that the result at the end really is "She/he loves me" (even if you have to pull out two petals at once). Then ask innocently if this statement really is true.

64

A declaration of love does not always have to take place before the first kiss. You could postpone it till after the second, third or thousandth kiss – if you are surer by then that the other person really is interested in you.

He covers me with kisses
from his mouth.
His love is sweeter than wine.
(The Old Testament)

Do you own a computer? With a suitable
word processor, create the cover sheet
of a fictional newspaper with the following
heading: "Sensation! (Your name) loves
(your beloved's name)!" Present this to the
partner of your dreams at a suitable occasion.

A little word of advice: Don't make
up stories about yourself in order
to win another person's love. Your "fib"
will soon be exposed, because in
the long run you can't pretend to be
someone that you aren't.

67

68

For especially courageous women: invite the object of your desire to your home. Welcome him in a see-through negligee or bathrobe beneath which you are naked and seduce the man you love. You can declare your love while you're doing this.

A declaration of love of the "magic" kind: put some sugar in a matchbox. Stick paper onto the box on which you have written several "love spells". Present the box with the following words to the object of your desire: "I wish that you would eat this so that you will love me as much as I love you."

70

A naughty declaration of love for women: buy a packet of colourful condoms and wrap it in gift paper. Present this gift to the person you love and say, "I hope that we will use up this packet as quickly as possible. I love you."

71

My heart does not rest,
Because your love
Has aroused it
With such longing
That it can only rest in you.
(Nikolaus of Kues)

Tell your beloved about the
difficulties you have sleeping. If he
or she asks for the reason, say,
"I can't sleep anymore because I can
only think of you since we met."

72

Sleep is love, watching is life.
In life you belong to the day,
In love you belong to the night.
(Johann Wilhelm Ritter)

74

Do you think handicrafts are old-fashioned? Not if you can declare your love in this way! Knit a jumper or a scarf and work in a knitted "I love you" (you could also embroider this, if you think this would be too difficult), and present your work to the person you love. Even if he will never wear it – it will still be a pleasant memory.

75

Our life consists of love,
And to love no more is to live no more.
(George Sand)

The marriage proposal

The marriage proposal is the most beautiful declaration of love possible – after all, it means that you would like to spend the rest of your life with the other person (even though it often works out different in reality). There are thousands of ways of proposing marriage. A few are listed on the following pages.

76

Take your partner out for a sumptuous meal – to a restaurant, for example, that you rarely visit. Order champagne or at least a good sparkling wine; of course, the meal should also be something special. When your partner asks what the reason for the celebration is (and this question is bound to arise!) this is the time to pop the question.

77

A humorous form of marriage proposal: buy a small tent and give it to the person you love, saying, "Unfortunately I couldn't afford more, but maybe you would still like to share my humble abode as my wife/husband in future?"

78

Surprise your partner by visiting the place where you first met or where you kissed for the first time. At this important place, you could propose in the following way: "Here we met/kissed for the first time. Since then my life has become much happier. I would be happier still if you married me."

79

Is there a local radio station where you live? Maybe you could ask if it is possible to pop the question to your partner on radio. However, you must make sure that your partner is listening when the proposal is being broadcast.

80

Give your partner a book with love poems. On the first page write – as a dedication, so to speak – "I love you and would like to spend the rest of my life with you. Will you marry me?"

81

Rather a cheeky marriage proposal: take the ring-pull from a can of coke and put it on your partner's finger with the words, "Unfortunately I couldn't afford anything better – but I hope you will still marry me."

A holiday together is the ideal time for a marriage proposal. In the evening, go to the beach with your partner and watch the sun set. In such a romantic mood it won't be difficult to find the right words for a proposal.

82

83

Give your partner a trip with a balloon as a present. High above the clouds, say "Together with you I always feel on cloud nine, not only now. To make sure it stays this way I would like you to become my wife/husband."

84

For puzzle enthusiasts: draw a picture puzzle or a crossword that expresses your desire to get married. This is not that easy but you will manage if you use your imagination. Your partner will now have to solve this puzzle, which you give to him or her nicely wrapped.

85

Get hold of the wedding march on CD or cassette. Play it on a suitable occasion, for example after a romantic meal or when you are lying on the bed together, dreaming. If your partner now asks you what the music is supposed to mean, you will probably only need to smile and put your arms around your beloved ...

86

For men: when friends get married, make sure (by arranging this with the bride) that your partner catches the flower bouquet. According to folklore, the girl who catches the bridal bouquet will be the next to get married. Once your partner has caught the bouquet, you should immediately propose to her.

87

Give your partner the most treasured of all
your belongings as a present. Tell him that you
are giving him this important item because
you want to share everything with him – in the
future, too. Then propose to him.

88

True love makes the thought of death something mundane, bearable, without fright, a simple parable, or a price that one gladly pays for certain things. (Stendhal)

89

In the evening, stand outside your partner's bedroom window. Throw a stone or two so that he or she opens the window and now sing a serenade. After this, pop the important question.

It is no longer fashionable to climb into your girlfriend's room with the aid of a ladder, because times have changed and you can ring the doorbell instead. But for a marriage proposal this old custom is ideal. Throw a few stones at her window so that she opens it, and climb in. Then you could say, "You can see what hardships I take upon myself to come and see you. So that I don't have to suffer any longer – would you like to marry me?"

90

91

How could I doubt
your love, since I am
conscious of my own so
fervently!
(Franz Grillparzer)

92

How about an ad in the paper to tell the whole world what your partner means to you? However, you should propose to your partner personally once he or she has read it.

93

A marriage proposal can also be completely spontaneous –
at an especially blissful moment you are experiencing with your
partner. Maybe you notice in the middle of a snowball fight or
in an everyday situation that you love your partner so much you
would like to grow old with him or her. It doesn't matter when
– give free rein to your feelings!

94

Are you familiar with the Chinese fortune cookies that contain a little note with a "prophecy"? Why not bake some cookies like this yourself? On each note you could write the question, "Will you marry me?"

95

Write a love poem to say how much your partner means to you. Then recite it to your beloved at the next suitable occasion. Afterwards you could say, "Now you know how important you are to me. Will you marry me?"

96

The classical marriage proposal: the man buys rings for himself
and for his beloved – however, these are not the wedding rings. When he
puts the ring on her finger, he asks if she will marry him.

97

Do you have an old car?
Paint your marriage proposal
on the car body and then
drive to your partner's flat.

If your car isn't quite that old, you
could put a sign on its roof which
expresses your love and your desire
to get married.

98

99

Buy some coloured chalk and on a sunny day write
the following on the road surface where your partner lives:
"I love you, (partner's name). Will you marry me?" You
should be present when your beloved reads this message!

100

Do you both like scuba diving? Then you could propose under water - of course, the ideal place would be a true diver's paradise! Since you can't talk under water, you will have to explain to your partner with gestures (and maybe by presenting him or her with a ring?) that you would like to marry him or her.

101

After a steamy night of love, write your marriage proposal with lipstick on your body. Of course you could also "paint" two interconnecting rings and a question mark on your body with cream from an aerosol tin. Afterwards your partner can make a meal of you!

102

Love is not a solo.
Love is a duet.
If it dwindles for one,
the song ceases.
(Adalbert von Chamisso)

103

If you would like to take the risk, have your partner's name tattooed on your body. Show the tattoo to your partner and say, "My love for you goes under my skin – will you marry me?"

104

Are you an Internet freak and do you and your partner live
in different towns or cities? Meet your beloved in a chatroom.
In a private conversation, you can then propose via data line.

105

Of course, you could also propose via e-mail, but in this case your proposal should be something very original. You could, for example, send the wedding march as an attachment or a photo of the two of you which you have processed on computer in such a way that you are dressed as bride and groom.

106

If you have a dog, you can use it to play Cupid: write your marriage proposal on a sheet of paper, wrap it in a plastic container and let your dog take this to your partner. You can be sure that it will be a big surprise!

107

How about a marriage proposal in rhyme? Show what a great poet you are – of course, the lines should exactly fit your situation. Recite your poem for your beloved on a suitable occasion – if you kneel down, you will impress even more.

108

A gateau surprise (maybe for your partner's birthday?): get hold of a huge plastic cream cake that is large enough for a person to fit inside – you could possibly get this from a party organiser. Sit inside the cake and have it taken to your partner's place at a suitable moment. Jump out and say, "Here is my present. Will you marry me?"

109

Wear something really sexy when you jump out of the cake – the surprise will be all the greater!

110

Love is the desire to give, not to receive.
(Bertolt Brecht)

111

A classical marriage proposal: the man puts on his best suit, gives his beloved a bunch of roses and goes down on his knees to ask her if she would like to marry him. Wouldn't that be the right idea for you? It is certainly romantic!

112

If you're pretty sure that your partner will say "yes", you could give him or her a ticket (or a voucher) to fly to Las Vegas, the wedding paradise. You could then get married there and spend your honeymoon in the US.

113

Paris is one of the world's most beautiful cities for lovers, so why not propose to your partner at one of the many romantic spots on the banks of the Seine?

114

Venice, too, is not just an
ideal place for a honeymoon, but
also for a marriage proposal
in front of a romantic backdrop.

Do you and your partner love going to the disco? Why not ask at your favourite disco if you could propose via microphone. First of all let the DJ play a song that has a special meaning for you and your partner, and then go up to the microphone to declare your love in front of everybody.

115

116

For disco freaks who don't like the limelight quite
as much: it is enough to ask the DJ to play "your song".
Take your partner in your arms when the music
is playing, draw him or her close to you and propose.

117

Organise a video evening just for yourself and your partner and watch the most enjoyable scenes from your life together so far. At the end of the show you could say, for example, "I would like to experience many more moments such as these together with you. Will you marry me?"

The great happiness in love consists in finding peace in another heart.
(Julie de Lespinasse)

118

119

A dramatic performance for all who like this type of thing: dress up as a pirate with an eye patch, frilly shirt and sabre. Then kidnap your beloved from her place of work (you should arrange this beforehand with her boss) and take her to your boat – no matter if it is a rowing boat or a yacht. After this successful abduction, you go down on your knees and ask your beloved for her hand in marriage.

120

How about a paper chase as a marriage proposal: tell your partner that you have a present for him or her but that he or she must look for it – hints as to where it can be found are given in the course of a paper chase; he or she must then assemble these notes to make up a sentence. Write the words "Darling, will you marry me?" individually on pieces of paper along with information as to where the next note can be found. Once your partner has found all these notes, he or she can assemble your marriage proposal – you should be standing near him or her (maybe with a bunch of roses) and repeat the proposal.

121

Rent a boat – a sailing boat or a rowing boat – and invite your partner aboard. Take a bottle of champagne along with you and propose to your partner on the high seas (which of course could be a lake or a river) in a romantic fashion – far away from all the hustle and bustle on land.

122

For men: take your partner to a kids' playground (provided that your partner wants to have children of her own). Watch the hustle and bustle and say at the right moment, "Please start a family with me – marry me!"

123

For women: accompany your darling to a soccer match of his favourite club. Arrange with the stadium announcer that you propose to your beloved during the half-time break (you will have to find a pretext to get away). The stadium management will no doubt be obliging.

124

Have a friend make a video film of yourself in which you propose to your darling. Give him or her this video as a present and watch it together. Make sure you have some champagne ready!

A cassette you have recorded yourself or a CD you have burned with songs about marriage are sure to be understood as a hint when you give it to your partner.

125

126

If your partner still doesn't understand your intentions when he or she listens to this CD or cassette, you will have to be more direct and sing into his/her ear, "Will you marry me?"

127

That is love's magic power, that it
ennobles what is touched by its breath,
as the sun, whose golden rays will
transform even thunderclouds into gold.
(Franz Grillparzer)

128

Give your partner an album with the best photos of both of you as a present. It could also contain photos documenting your lives from childhood to the present day. The last photo should be a collage of the two of you as bride and groom. Underneath write in gold, "Will you marry me?"

129

Invite your beloved to a puppet show, where you will be the puppeteer. The two of you are the main characters. With the puppets, re-enact one of the most memorable occasions of your life together. At the end, have the puppet that represents you propose to the other puppet. Then come out from behind the puppet theatre and repeat your question.

Of course, your "puppet image" could also pose the question directly from the puppet theatre to your partner. While doing this, gradually emerge from behind the theatre.

130

131 Give your partner a book with blank pages as a present. If he or she asks in surprise what this is supposed to mean, say "This book is reserved for all the wonderful events of our married life. Please marry me!"

132

To worship the beloved
is the nature of the lover.
(Friedrich Schlegel)

133

Attach a cardboard or plastic heart to your shirt, pullover or T-shirt. Present it to your partner with the words "I am giving you my heart. Will you marry me?"

134

A casual marriage proposal can also have its attraction: at a moment when he or she is least expecting it (for example, while doing the dishes), simply ask your partner if he or she would like to marry you.

135

It's a hot summer's day. You are both lying on the beach or in the swimming pool. Put your hands on your partner's back. With your finger, write the individual letters of the question "Will you marry me?" on your partner's back. He or she now has to guess what you have written.

136

For somewhat more courageous people, but also for romantics: on a warm day, look for a quiet spot outside in nature where you can make love undisturbed. Afterwards, have a romantic picnic during which you propose to your partner.

The greatest happiness apart from loving:
declaring one's love.
(André Gide)

137

138

Surprise your beloved with strawberries in winter and other such delicacies that you normally don't allow yourself. Celebrate your very own private party and propose to your partner.

Buy a tandem and give it to your
partner as a present, saying
"I would like to go everywhere together
with you in future. Please marry me."

139

Give your beloved a cuddly toy. Put a paper roll around its neck on which you have written your marriage proposal, "Just like this cuddly toy, I would only like to cuddle you in future – please marry me!"

140

141

For unconventional people: a bunch of wildflowers isn't really anything special, but very beautiful. So go out and pick some wildflowers. Present them to your partner and propose marriage.

142

Give your partner a picture of two lovers. It could be a photo or an art reproduction. Write your proposal on the back of the picture.

143

If you enjoy writing, you could write several short love stories. Write down how you and your partner met and grew to love each other – the end of this story would be your wedding.

Enter these love stories in the computer and print them out so that you can have them bound as a little book (perhaps you could also do this yourself). Having read your love story, at the latest, your partner will understand...

145

Do you remember the children's angling game with magnets? Play this game with your partner, who doesn't know that you have also hidden two rings among the fish. When your partner fishes out one of the rings, propose to him or her.

I have always loved you,
Still love you today,
And will love you in all eternity.
(Ludwig Uhland)

146

147

Do you and your partner enjoy hiking in the mountains? What could be more beautiful than asking your partner on a mountaintop if he or she will marry you!

148

As a present, give your partner a dance course especially for brides and grooms who want to learn how to dance before the wedding. Your partner should understand this hint without any further explanation.

149

A marriage proposal in the snow is something very special. It doesn't matter if you propose in the snowfields, on the toboggan run, during a winter walk or after a snowball fight – the white splendour will give it just the right romantic touch.

150

For men: propose to your partner when she feels that she is not looking her best – because she isn't wearing make-up, has just woken up or hasn't yet washed her hair. Tell her how much you love here even when she doesn't find herself especially attractive, and top this by asking her to marry you.

Declarations of love
to your partner

The initial phase of infatuation, when you constantly assure your partner of your love, soon gives way to deeper feelings of tenderness and security (assuming of course you stay together). Unfortunately, in everyday life we often neglect to show our partner just how much we love him or her. This is a pity; after all, it is often the small loving gestures that make life with your partner so endearing and prevent a humdrum routine from developing. So show your love for your partner from time to time!

151

Go and watch a love film at the cinema with your
partner, hold hands and kiss in the dark like young lovers
do. An evening at the cinema such as this will help liven
up even a long-standing partnership. And who knows
– maybe it will develop into a really sensual evening…

Roses speak the language
of love. Give your beloved
a long-stemmed red rose
– or better still, present him or
her with a whole bunch!

152

If you get up before your partner, leave a small note on the kitchen table in the morning with a loving message such as "I'm already looking forward to seeing you", or "Without you, the day will really drag out". No matter whether you have known each other for a long time or if you've just met – such a message is bound to make your partner's day!

153

154

It is also a nice idea to write a love message with lipstick on the mirror, where it will definitely not your beloved's notice. However, you should be prepared to clean the mirror afterwards.

155

It is a pleasant surprise for your darling if he or she finds a declaration of love in his or her car, when setting off to work in the morning. You could, for example, fasten a note to the steering wheel on which you write, "Please drive carefully – I would like to have you around for a long time yet!"

156

In the morning, before work, put a photo of yourself in your darling's wallet (maybe even an erotic one?) without him noticing it. On the back, you could write, "I love you – come back to me soon."

157

For women: a little erotic surprise for your partner is sure to spice up your love life. Put an item of lingerie on the driver's seat of his car or hide it in his briefcase. This, together with a note saying, "At home there's a surprise waiting for you," will add some zest to your relationship even if you've already been living together for several years.

158

Does your partner tend to be grumpy in the morning? Wake him gently with a few caresses and some loving words. Your day will immediately start on a better note.

A few caresses before getting up (without going all the way) will increase the anticipation of seeing your partner again in the evening.

159

160

Give your partner a real treat. Fill the bath for him or her, add a fragrant bath essence and massage your partner's back while he or she is sitting in the bath. If you feel like it, you could join your partner – who knows what could happen then?

161

If your partner complains of a headache, offer a head massage. Gently massage the forehead, scalp and – still more gently – the neck. This is very relaxing, and it feels good too. Maybe you could even pamper him or her with a few kisses now and then?

162

If you have to get up before your partner, try not to wake him or her. This can also be a sign of love and respect, especially if your partner likes to lie in.

163

True love remains ever true to itself, whether it be granted all or denied all.
(Johann Wolfgang von Goethe)

164

For men: give your partner the perfume she has been wanting for a long time, even if you don't especially like it.

For women: wear the perfume that you really like, but which your partner detests, only when you're not together with him.

165

Always show your appreciation of your partner's declarations of love (whether they be in the form of words, gestures or gifts), even if they are sometimes made in a somewhat clumsy manner. This in return will show your partner how much you love him or her.

166

167

Pay your partner a compliment about his or her looks, especially when he or she doesn't feel very attractive at the time.

For women: if your partner is a soccer fan, go and see a match with him occasionally, even if you don't particularly enjoy it.

168

169

For men: do without the soccer broadcast if your wife would like to watch something else, but especially if she would prefer doing something else with you.

170

In the age of e-mail and Internet, love letters might be a little old-fashioned; on the other hand, they are a wonderful way of telling your partner how much you like him or her. A love letter is a special surprise if you have already been together with your partner for a long time.

171

Try to take a day off work on your partner's birthday. This gesture will show him or her how much he or she means to you.

Bring a bottle of champagne home with you without any particular reason and say, "Darling, let's celebrate our love tonight."

172

173

If your partner suffers from stress at work, help him relax properly in the evening. Take a walk together, have a nice meal, talk about pleasant things or simply put your arms around him or her.

174

Listen to your partner when he or she has problems and would like to talk about them. Even if you can't be of much help, it at least shows your concern.

175

It is not possible to simply caress problems away, but you can at least try. Be gentle towards your partner if he or she isn't feeling well for whatever reason.

176

Try and cheer up your partner with some loving words if he or she seems depressed. When your partner seems stressed or suffers from problems, declare your love, for example, "Even if you feel bad, I'm here for you. Together we will master all problems – because we love each other."

177

Love also means forgiveness. If your partner has offended you – maybe even unintentionally – you shouldn't sulk. You can show your displeasure, but you should also relent. You could show your desire for reconciliation in a special way – by seducing your partner.

178

Grant your partner certain liberties – after all, trust is also a sign of love. Be happy with your partner if he or she has experienced something pleasant, even if you weren't there at the time.

179

The God of love led me to you.
(Giuseppe Verdi)

180

If your partner flirts with another person, show your jealousy (but only in moderation!). This will show your partner that you still find him or her desirable. However, make sure you keep your jealousy under control – exaggerated jealousy can be very restrictive.

For your partner's sake, you should occasionally abstain from bad habits such as smoking, if he or she asks you to do so. This will show your partner how much you respect him or her, and this is also a kind of declaration of love.

181

182

For men: give your wife an item of clothing that she especially likes, even if you find it rather unflattering on her. However, don't tell her that you don't like it.

For women: occasionally wear an item of clothing for him that he adores, even if you don't particularly like it.

183

Give your partner your heart as a present – for example in the form of a big gingerbread heart. At the fair, you will find gingerbread hearts with loving words galore. How about "Forever yours"?

184

185

Give your partner nicknames. These should be loving, but one thing is especially important: they should appeal not only to you, but also to your partner.

186

Why not show that you love your partner in front of other people? Why not kiss him or her in the street? You probably did this quite often when you first got together and you didn't feel ashamed about it then.

This is one of the nicest declarations of love that you could give to a woman who is longing for a child: simply say, "Throw those stupid contraceptives away," and then make love to her on her day of ovulation.

187

188

To say that it is impossible to always love the same woman
is as tasteless as saying that a famous artist needs several
violins to play a piece of music and to create a magic melody.
(Honoré de Balzac)

Tell your partner the merits that he or she has in comparison with other people and that you especially love about him or her.

189

190

Write a love poem for your partner and put it under his or her pillow.

191

Does your partner love dancing, whereas you can't dance at all? Attend a dancing course (maybe even without your partner knowing about it) and surprise him or her by tripping the light fantastic together.

In an everyday situation, whisper "I love you" in your partner's ear – just as you did at the start of your relationship. It will be a wonderful surprise for him or her.

192

193

For women: seduce your partner after a long working day. Wear attractive clothes (perhaps some enticing lingerie), use some exciting perfume, pour a glass of wine for your partner and yourself and then slowly start to pamper him.

For courageous women, but also for men: seduce your partner with a skilful striptease, which isn't really that difficult at all. Simply rehearse a little in front of the mirror – your partner is bound to overlook any minor "faults" in your dance of seduction and will be thrilled.

194

195

Arouse your partner's curiosity for what he can expect in the evening when you want to perform your striptease. Phone him at work and tell him that a surprise is waiting for him when he comes home.

196

A special kind of declaration of love: do you and your partner have different ideas about your holidays, and has this frequently been the cause of differences between you? When you're planning your next holidays, simply agree to his or her ideas without complaining – simply because you love him or her!

197

Call your beloved at work during the day and play a love song over the phone.

198

Reciting a classical love poem during a phone call could also brighten up your partner's day.

199

If your partner is very open in sexual matters, you could give him a lot of pleasure by telling him over the phone just what you would like to do with him if he was with you at the time.

Has your partner ever dreamt of making love on the beach? Fulfil this wish on your next holiday.

200

201

During sex, tell your partner when you like something especially. On the one hand, this is a wonderful declaration of love, and on the other, he or she will also get to know what you like.

202

The whole art of love seems to me to consist of saying what the magic of the moment requires, that is, to follow one's heart. But one shouldn't assume this is easy. (Stendhal)

203

Praise your partner more often instead of criticising him or her. This kills two birds with one stone: firstly, your partner feels loved and accepted by you, and secondly, your partner is bound to repeat what he or she was praised for in order to earn renewed praise.

204

If your partner is very keen to see a particular film, watch it together with him or her even if doesn't really interest you. He or she is bound to understand this kind of declaration of love.

Does your partner love operas or operettas, and you don't? You should still occasionally give your partner a ticket to the opera and accompany him or her.

205

206

Making love on the floor is a good way to liven up a dull evening. Spread out a blanket, ask your partner to lie down beside you and start caressing him or her. This unusual place for lovemaking will liven up your love life.

207

For men: give your partner a day without the children.
She could, for example, go shopping in peace or
meet old girlfriends while you look after the youngsters.

208

If your partner is stressed, give him a wellness weekend where he or she can recover from the daily grind – it doesn't have to be a special occasion.

Let your partner go on holiday without you for a week. He or she will understand your trust as a proof of love.

209

If your partner asks you about previous amorous adventures, you should tell him or her about them. However, you should never make the mistake of comparing him or her with previous partners; instead you should emphasise your partner's merits – without criticising or denigrating ex-partners.

210

211

If you and your partner meet a one-time boyfriend or girlfriend of yours, introduce your new partner in a polite manner. Show your previous partner that you and your new partner now belong together by putting your arm around him or her or by holding your partner's hand. Your partner is bound to value this as a declaration of love.

212

If a former boyfriend or
girlfriend starts flirting with
you at a party, be friendly
but firm and leave him or her
standing there. If your new
partner notices this, this is the
nicest declaration of love you
could give him.

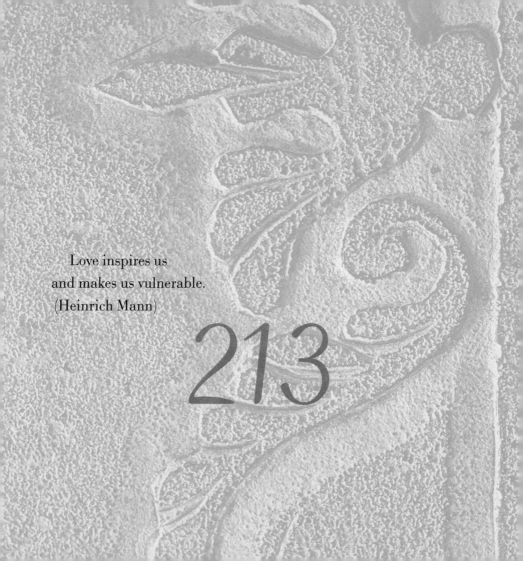

Love inspires us
and makes us vulnerable.
(Heinrich Mann)

213

214

You aren't married yet? Remember – one of the nicest declarations of love in the world is the proposal of marriage, especially if your partner isn't expecting it.

A gastronomic declaration of love: prepare your partner's favourite meal even if you don't especially like it. Don't cook meals that he or she detests.

215

Give your partner a surprise
birthday party. Prepare the party
without your partner noticing
it and secretly invite guests that your
partner especially likes.

216

217

As a surprise for the birthday party bake a cake (or buy one) with a loving message.

218

A declaration of love as a welcome after a humdrum working day: how about putting up a (self-made) banner above your door with the words, "Welcome home, Queen/King of my heart."

219

It doesn't matter how long ago you got married – surprise your partner with a second honeymoon. Plan a romantic journey just for the two of you. If you have children, this trip doesn't need to be long, but you should still treat yourselves.

At the weekend, serve your partner breakfast in bed. A red rose in a little vase is a must. And if the bread crumbs don't bother you, you could have an erotic "dessert".

220

Think up something new in bed
now and again. It doesn't have to
be anything spectacular, but it should
liven up your love life.

221

Accept a 'no' in bed.
If your partner doesn't like
something or other,
you shouldn't be insistent.

222

223

Invite your partner to go dancing – it doesn't matter whether it's the discotheque next door or a dance hall. Make sure that it is a carefree evening: organise a baby-sitter, order a taxi so that neither of you has to drive, and only have eyes for your partner.

224

Try and see your partner as you did at
the start of your relationship. Remember all
the little characteristics and qualities of
your partner that used to fascinate you back
then. These characteristics (or at least
some of them) arc bound to be still there.
Tell your partner what you loved about
him or her back then and still love today.

If your partner is in a difficult situation you should give him or her your support, even if you think he or she isn't in the right. Support your partner in front of others, and demonstrate your affection and loyalty. You can always criticise him or her at home in private.

225

226

It is love's sacred godly ray
That strikes the soul and fires,
When like and like meet.
There is no resistance and no choice:
Humans shall not undo what's bonded in heaven.
(Friedrich von Schiller)

Every partnership has to weather a big storm at one time or another. Don't immediately throw in the towel; try instead to save your love.

227

228

After an argument it's time to make up again: take your partner firmly in your arms, whisper loving words into his or her ear and ask for forgiveness if necessary.

Symbolically give your partner a thousand kisses. List on a piece of paper what kind of kisses these are, for example: 0 brotherly kisses, 12 loving kisses, 35 hot kisses, 157 passionate kisses and so on ...

229

230

For men without a beard: a regular shave can also be a proof of love. A five o'clock shadow might look masculine, but isn't very pleasant for your darling if your stubble scratches her face.

231

Walk through town with your partner, holding hands. This shows that you belong together – even if almost everybody knows this already. This tender gesture can say more than a thousand words.

232

During a warm summer shower take your partner's hand, rush outside and run and dance with him or her in the rain. Kiss your partner and feel how the warm rain mingles with your kisses.

Love is taking the dog
for a walk even when
it is your partner's turn.

233

Wash your partner's car
without him or her having
asked for it. Car enthusiasts
will especially regard
this as a declaration of love.

234

235

If you are a non-smoker, show your partner that you love him by fetching cigarettes for him (at least occasionally) when he has run out. Let him turn one room of your flat into a "smoker's parlour" (but only if you don't have children!).

236

You should give up smoking if your partner is a non-smoker. On the one hand, this doesn't force him or her to smoke passively, and on the other, you will probably prolong your life and thus the time that you can spend with your partner.

Is your partner's car dusty or dirty? Write "I love you" with your finger on the dusty paintwork and add a large heart. To prevent any misunderstandings, you should sign this message with your name.

237

Provide a cosy atmosphere when your partner is ill – with fluffy blankets, soft pillows and warm tea.

238

239

If your partner is feeling sick, show your love and care by not eating the most delicious dishes right in front of him or her. Try not to talk about eating at all, but instead prepare some tea for your partner that calms the stomach.

For men: show understanding for your partner's urge to telephone. After all, it goes without saying that women have to talk for hours when they have bought a new piece of clothing.

240

241

For women: accept that
he has to meet his friends in the
pub for a beer occasionally,
so that they can demonstrate to
each other their qualities as
a premier division soccer coach.
Even though one beer usually
becomes ten, you shouldn't
let this bother you too much.

242

For women: be understanding if your partner doesn't ask for instructions when he has taken the wrong road. Men simply have to prove that they have enough sense of direction to find the way without somebody else's help.

For men: don't make a fuss when your partner reacts more sensitively around the time of menstruation. Simply take her in your arms if she starts crying again for no apparent reason.

243

244

Doubt that the stars are fine,
Doubt that the sun doth move,
Doubt truth to be a liar,
But never doubt I love.
(William Shakespeare)

If your partner is from a different country, you should learn his or her mother tongue. In any case, you should collect information on the country's culture and typical customs – not just in case you visit your partner's home country, but also to show your interest in his or her origins.

245

Read your partner's favourite book so that you can have a discussion with him or her about it, even if you really think this would be a waste of time.

246

247

Try and control your moods when you are together with your partner. Most people tend to take their moods out on their loved ones, but this certainly is no proof of love.

248

Accept your partner's occasional bad moods. Try and cheer him or her up so that he or she can relax. But if your partner turns this down and would rather be alone, you should accept this without being offended.

249

If you wanted to be on your own for a while because of
a bad mood, you should approach your partner once it has
blown over, take him on your arms, give him a big kiss
and ask for forgiveness for your moodiness. Thank him for
accepting you the way you are.

How about a partner massage? This is not as difficult as you might think. However, you should not massage bones, and you must stop immediately if your partner finds it painful for. Use a fragrant oil such as almond oil for the massage.

250

251

A partner massage shouldn't be too rough; rather look at it as a caress for your partner's soul. And maybe you could intersperse a different type of caress now and then, so that the whole occasion eventually takes an erotic turn.

For men: if your partner tells you she is pregnant, you should be happy with her – even if you are afraid of taking responsibility for a child.

252

253

Accompany your partner to the birth preparation classes. You might find this boring, but you will be proving to your partner that you take an interest in her and her pregnancy.

Show understanding for your partner during her pregnancy – even if her moods sometimes seem unbearable. After all, you know how hormones can play up…

254

255

Put a little note into your partner's trouser or jacket pocket – where he's bound to find it. Write a brief declaration of love on this note. Especially if you have been together for a long time, this is bound to liven up the love in your partnership.

256

A love message via SMS isn't just for young people. You should especially send an SMS when your partner isn't expecting to receive a loving message from you on his mobile phone.

257

Why not put an ad in the paper, in which you tell your beloved and the entire world how much you love him or her; it doesn't have to be a special occasion. But make sure your partner actually gets around to reading it.

Do you have a weekend relationship? Why not surprise
your partner with a visit in the middle of the week?
You should, however, be sure that he or she is at home,
so that you don't make the trip in vain.

258

259

Give your partner a mobile phone
as a present, so that you can get
in touch with him or her at any time.
To avoid giving the impression that
you want to monitor him or her,
you should only phone at previously
arranged times.

260

If you live further apart, you could send your partner a surprise parcel which could contain chocolates in the shape of hearts, for example. It should always be accompanied by a love letter, even if it is only a short one.

261

During a candlelight dinner, remind your partner of the time you got to know each other and the early days of your relationship. Tell him how beautiful you found this new love, but then say that it has now become even more beautiful – perhaps because you now feel much closer to your partner than you did at that time.

262

Nor dare I question with my jealous thought
Where you may be or your affairs suppose
But like a sad slave stay and think of nought
Save where you are, how happy you make those.
(William Shakespeare)

263

For men: you should at least occasionally do the dishes, if your partner hates this chore. She will understand this declaration of love without the need for words.

264

Buy a dishwasher so that neither of you has to do the dishes. "Present" the dishwasher as a gift and say, "Now we shall have more time for each other at last."

265 Go for an ice cream together. Order a portion for two (which is available in most ice-cream parlours) to show that you share everything with your partner.

For women: pay your partner compliments about his prowess as a lover. This is probably one of the nicest declarations of love and it will be an incentive for him to continue to do his best in bed in the future.

266

267

Accept his friends/her girlfriends even if you don't especially like them. Do something together with your partner and those friends. In most cases, it will be important for your partner for you to get on with his/her friends.

Try and get on a good footing with your partner's family.
In general, it will probably be important for your partner
that you get on with his or her parents and siblings. After all, you
might become part of this family or maybe you already are.

268

Attend your partner's family's celebrations together with him or her. This shows that you are interested in your partner, his/her family and therefore his/her past. And maybe you are your partner's only bright spot during these often boring "duties".

269

270

Give your partner a special present without waiting for a special occasion: a balloon trip with a picnic above cloud nine. If your partner doesn't have a fear of flying, you are sure to have a great time.

271

On your anniversary, make a thank-you speech for your partner because you are together. Emphasise the best aspects of your partnership, without forgetting to mention the darker moments. Focus on how you managed to overcome the difficult times in your relationship with a combined effort.

272

For all lovers in a long-term relationship: at a special moment
ensure your partner that you still love him/her as much as
on the first day (or possibly even more) – even though it might
not seem like this sometimes.

273

I love and don't tell you,
and do you love me? I don't ask you.
I'd like to ask but I don't dare,
I love and say nothing and don't complain.
(Hoffmann von Fallersleben)

274

On your anniversary pretend that you've just met. This will
no doubt be a special declaration of love for your partner. In addition,
this old "game" is bound to revive old love.

Why not act as a "human hot water bottle" when your partner feels cold. Cover him/her and yourself with a blanket and then start cuddling your partner lovingly.

275

276

Place a photo of your partner on your desk – at the office and at home. In addition, put a photo of him or her in your wallet.

277

If your partner has to go on a business trip or if you are separated for a short time for some other reason, give him or her a cuddly toy. On the one hand, it is intended to protect him or her from bad "influences" (other men or women) and, on the other, to remind your partner that you are thinking of him or her.

Do you or your partner love phoning? Do you spend hours on the Internet? Give your partner an ISDN connection with two lines so that both of you can satisfy your passion without getting in each other's way.

278

For him: never ask your partner how much a piece of clothing cost (even if she withdrew the money from your account). Tell her instead how beautiful she looks wearing it.

279

280

Take a walk together, but don't just walk next to each other – put your arm around your partner, just as you did when you first got together. It is nice for your partner and for yourself to feel the warmth of the other person and to know that he or she is there for you.

Never ask your partner do to something that he or she can't fulfil. For example, you will never manage to turn someone chaotic into a neat and tidy person. Accept this and love your partner just the way he or she is.

281

282

If your parents criticise your partner, always stand up for him or her to prove your loyalty – especially if he or she is present while being criticised, and even if you actually agree with your parents' criticism. However, you don't have to tell anyone else that apart from your partner.

283

If there are shooting stars in the night sky, watch them together with your partner and make a wish. If your partner asks what you wished for, hesitate a little, before you say, "I wish that we will always love one another."

284

Do I love you?
Ask the stars.
(Karl Herolssohn)

285

Laugh at your partner's jokes – especially
if no one else laughs at them. This shows
your partner that you are standing up
for him (even if you didn't really find the
joke funny yourself). In addition, your
partner won't feel that he has made a fool
of himself – after all, it is embarrassing
if no one laughs at the joke you've just told.

286

If your partner cries over something that has happened, you shouldn't hesitate to cry together, even if you feel that you should rather console your partner. Crying in itself is a consolation, but even more comforting is the knowledge that there is a person with you who understands and shares your feelings.

287

Don't hide your tears from your partner – no matter why you are crying. This shows your partner that you trust him or her and that you don't have to hide your weakness. Can there be a better proof of love?

288

If other people are laughing at your partner, don't join them. On the contrary: speak to the others about their bad behaviour (because this is what this is) and make a fool of them in this way.

289

The saying goes that malicious joy is the best joy, but in regard to your partner this is completely unfitting, because it can deeply hurt another person. Make sure you never show satisfaction at your partner's misfortunes.

Love has nothing to do with what you want to get –
only with that which you yourself want to give.
(Katherine Hepburn)

290

291

Surprise your partner with a phone call from work (maybe shortly after he rings you?). Tell him how much you are looking forward to seeing him again, how pleasant it is for you to at least hear his voice and how much you are missing him.

292

Give your partner some erotic lingerie made from a flattering material. When you make your choice, don't just go by your own taste but also think about that of your partner. If she prefers white underwear, whereas you prefer black, you should definitely choose white lingerie.

Never compare your partner with an unattainable ideal (what woman, for example, really does look like a super model?). If you have to make comparisons, they should be in favour of your partner.

293

Plan a weekend just for
yourself, your partner
and your love. Switch off the
telephone and doorbell, so
that you can't be disturbed.
Have breakfast in bed together,
make love and do all those
things together that you
normally don't have time for.

294

295

Fulfil one of your partner's dreams. It doesn't matter if this is an introductory course for hang gliding or a visit to Disneyland – just make it possible. Your partner is bound to understand this declaration of love.

Go on a surprise trip with your partner. Pack his or her suitcases, put them in your car, pick your partner up on Friday after work and drive to a place that you both like or that you have always wanted to visit. Of course, you mustn't say anything to your partner beforehand!

296

297

Buy new rings for both of you – they shouldn't replace your current friendship or wedding rings, but rather complement them.

298

Give your partner a ring with a special engraving. How about "Forever yours" or "Thank you for the wonderful years"? Perhaps you have your own secret code to say "I love you."

Plant a tree for your darling.
Tell her that your love will grow like
this tree in the years to come.

299

Don't attend a meeting with friends or sporting events if your partner doesn't feel well. Be there just for him or her.

300

301

Always defend your partner against attacks from other people – it doesn't matter where they come from, if they are justified or even if you think the same. Loyalty is an important demonstration of love in a partnership.

At no time are we more vulnerable to suffering than when we love.
(Sigmund Freud)

302

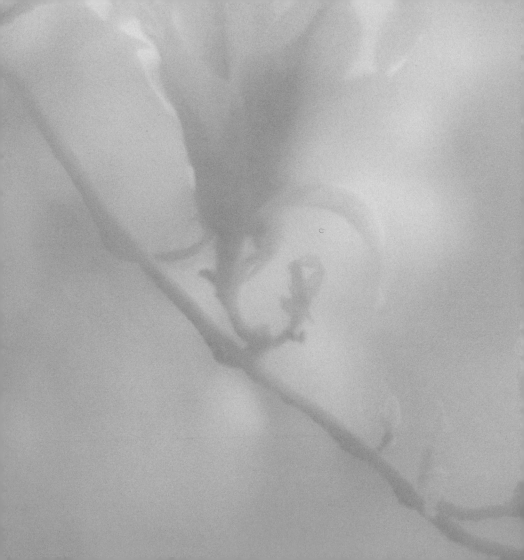

Dear parents

Most of us will probably find that we all too seldom show our parents just how much we love them. But when we really come to think about it, there is so much that we owe to our parents – which is reason enough to tell them you love them every now and then, no matter how.

303

When was the last time you gave your parents a hug? Is it some time ago? Then you should pluck up some courage and embrace them warmly. You can be sure that it will do your parents a lot of good.

304

If you live close to your parents, you should perhaps visit them more often – not just when you want something from them. It only has to be a short visit; after all, it is intended more as a loving gesture.

305

If your parents (or one parent) live in a retirement home, visit them regularly so that they have something to look forward to. If you only turn up occasionally on a Sunday between lunch and afternoon tea, your parents are sure to feel neglected.

Invite your parents out for a meal with you
(and perhaps also your family) even when there is
no special occasion. Your parents may well be
surprised at first if you have never done something
like this before, they are sure to enjoy it.

306

307

If you have children, you should make sure that they get to know their grandparents – in other words, your parents – well. Grandparents usually love their grandchildren and are always happy to see them.

Write a letter to your parents, expressing your gratitude for everything they have ever done for you.

308

309

Give your parents a special present: a trip to a place that they have always wanted to visit. Of course, they have to be physically fit for such an experience.

310

Always invite your parents for major holidays such as Christmas or Easter if you have enough room in your house. Remember how your parents always made these times so special for you.

Prepare a special surprise for your mother on Mother's Day: how about a present such as a weekend at a wellness resort?

311

312

Forgive your parents for their mistakes, and if possible forget them. Remember – your parents are probably too old to make any major changes in their lives.

313

Stand by your parents in difficult times. Let them 0know that you will be there for them even after the event if they need or want you.

314

Carry out tasks for your parents that they used to do for you – especially if they are no longer physically capable of doing these themselves. For instance, you could do the weekly washing for your parents, clean up their flat or at least ensure that someone, for example a cleaner, takes care of all these daily chores.

315

Bake your parents a cake or buy them a gingerbread heart which says "for the world's best Mum and Dad". You may find this a little silly at first, but your parents are sure to be delighted.

Look after your parents' pet when one of them is
ill or make sure that someone else takes care of
it if your parents are unable to do this themselves.

316

317

The Earth is freed through love
and is ennobled through actions.
(Johann Wolfgang von Goethe)

Always try and keep appointments that you
have arranged with your parents, even
if something "better" comes up beforehand.

318

Organise the things for your parents that they are no longer capable of or feel that they can no longer do themselves. For example, you could go to the local authorities for them, or do the weekly shopping or even sort out arguments with neighbours.

319

320

Be there for your parents if they become sick (especially if the illness is serious). It doesn't matter if you have to travel a long distance or even if you have to take time off work to see them.

If you do not live close to your parents, make sure to keep them informed of how their grandchildren are growing. Send them lots of photos and allow your children to talk with their grandparents on the telephone when they are old enough.

321

If your parents live far away from you, get them used to the idea of using modern communication media such as fax or e-mail. Give them a fax machine or pay for an Internet connection and show them how to use these. In this way you will be able to stay in contact much more easily.

322

Don't get annoyed with your parents when they still see the child in you. However old you may be, you are still your parents' child.

323

324

When we are young, love is more turbulent, but not as powerful as later in life.
(Heinrich Heine)

325

Surely one of the greatest signs of love you can show your parents is to take them into your home when they are no longer capable of looking after a household or if they need care. If this is not possible, find a place in a good retirement home or care facilities for them. Be especially careful when making your choice.

Talk with your parents about how enjoyable they made your childhood for you. Praise them, for example, for how much you always looked forward to the special occasions such Christmas or your birthday, but also for the fact that they were always there for you when you needed them even when they were very busy.

326

327

Console your parents when times are bad for them, just like they used to console you during your childhood. Stay overnight if you feel that your presence would help your parents to overcome their sadness.

Laugh together with your parents. The older you become, the more you will find you have in common with them – this also applies to humour.

328

329

Compliment your parents on their appearance, how fit they
are or how understanding they are towards modern youth
or whatever. Most parents love compliments from their children.

Don't hesitate to ask your parents' advice on how to bring up your own children. Even if you then decide not to take their advice, your parents at least feel as if they are being included in your family life – a wonderful token of your love.

330

My dearest child

Children are the most valuable thing in this world – after all, they are our future. So show your children more often just how much you love them. The more love a child experiences, the more it can express its own love later on in life. Perhaps this is a way to make the world a better place to live in...

331

The simplest way to show a baby love is to react immediately when it cries. By doing so you are strengthening its trust in you and the world.

332

You should take some time each day to spend cuddling your child (even a few minutes is enough). Lie down together with him or her on the settee, the floor or the bed and read a book together and cuddle up closely to one another.

333

Just like small children, teenagers also need your warmth and affection – even if they prefer to appear cool on the outside. So take your teenage son or daughter in your arms every day. However, make sure that you are alone – if others see you cuddling, your child is sure to feel embarrassed.

334

Take part in a baby massage course with your child.
These caresses do your baby the world of good and
show it just how much you love it. You can even massage your
child in this way when he or she is no longer a baby.

Older children also enjoy being massaged. Why not try it? Your touch is sure to relax your child.

335

336

A childhood of love can
provide against the
cold world for half a lifetime.
(Jean Paul)

Praise your children for things that they
have done especially well or which they are
particularly proud of, even if you don't
think the result is especially good. Praise
shows your children that you love them.

337

338

Make some time every day for your child – not just fifteen minutes or so, but a lot longer. During this time, occupy yourself intensively with your child, play with him, tell him stories, talk with him or simply listen to what he has to say to you.

339

Never talk uncharitably about your child to others. If the child gets wind of this he or she could lose trust in you.

340

Never compare your child with other children. Every child is special, has special characteristics and can do special things that other children of the same age cannot do.

341

Always give your children encouragement when they feel
that they cannot master a problem or a situation. Perhaps
you can explain how you managed to overcome similar situations
when you were that age.

342

We cannot mould children as we would wish; we must accept and love them as God gave them to us. (Johann Wolfgang von Goethe)

Console your child when he or she is not feeling well. Even older children need to be consoled in certain situations.

343

344

Cuts and bruises hurt. Stroke or "blow" the pain away and take your child in your arms if it has injured itself. You attention will soon make your child forget its pain.

345 Give your child a book that deals with love and affection. Write a dedication such as "I love you lots and lots."

346 When you have to leave your child on its own, write her a little note saying, "Back soon – and then we'll do something really nice together. Love, Mum/Dad".

347

Never force your child to do something that it really does not want to do – unless this is "really necessary". This includes such things as visits to the doctor and taking medication as well as being mindful of traffic.

Not every one of your children's wishes has to be fulfilled. However, at birthdays you should respect your child's wishes, even if you are not entirely happy with the choice of present – of course, this is assuming that finances allow the wish to be fulfilled.

348

Setting limits also shows your child that you love it. By laying down rules, you are structuring the child's world and giving it important orientation as to what is right and wrong.

349

350

Children and clocks should not
be constantly wound up.
We should also let them run down.
(Jean Paul)

Always take your child seriously, with all his or her fears, worries, needs and desires. There is a reason for all of these.

351

352

Sing your children a song that shows you love them. You could write this song yourself and express all your feelings in the lyrics.

Tell your children regularly that you love them. There is sure to be a suitable, very special moment each day.

353

354

Forgive your children when they oppose you and do exactly the opposite of that what you expect or have told them to do. It is only natural that children oppose their parents now and then.

355

Never use any form of violence towards your children. Even a "little slap" is not an adequate means of bringing up children, as you will then not be showing your child how to behave "properly" but only humiliating him or her.

356

Allow your children to have a private life – you do not have to know every little thing they do. In this way you will show your children that you trust them.

I believe that bringing up children
must be directed towards love.
(Astrid Lindgren)

357

358

When planning holidays, take your children's wishes and needs into account. They will then feel that you understand them and take them seriously. Besides, your holiday is sure to be more harmonious if your children have been allowed to take part in the decision-making process.

If you discover that your child is being bullied, sit down together and work out a solution to the problem.

359

360

Show your joy at your child's successes – regardless of whether these are "big" events in your child's life, such as when it takes its first steps, or smaller experiences that may not appear so important to you but which are very significant to your child.

Laugh together with your child at least once a day. You will see that laughter helps release any tensions there may be, and this will strengthen the bond between you.

361

Never tell your children that others could do something better than they can. Remember that you could not do everything perfectly when you were that age. Your child will find its own way.

362

363

Don't spoil your child's pleasure.
Even if you do not fully agree with his
behaviour, accept your child's decision.
Invite his friends around more often
– perhaps your concerns will be allayed
sooner than you thought possible.

364

When your child falls in love for the first time, be happy for your son or daughter. Try to ignore any "faults" you think the girl/boyfriend may have.

A child is a book from which we read
and in which we should write.
(Peter Rosegger)

365